SKYFIRE

By FRANK ASCH

HARCOURT BRACE & COMPANY

Orlando   Atlanta   Austin   Boston   San Francisco   Chicago   Dallas   New York
Toronto   London

This edition is published by special arrangement with Simon & Schuster
Books For Young Readers, a division of Simon & Schuster Inc.

Grateful acknowledgment is made to Simon & Schuster Books For Young
Readers, a Division of Simon & Schuster Inc. for permission to reprint
Skyfire by Frank Asch. Copyright © 1984 by Frank Asch.

Printed in the United States of America

ISBN 0-15-302118-7

4 5 6 7 8 9 10   035   97 96 95

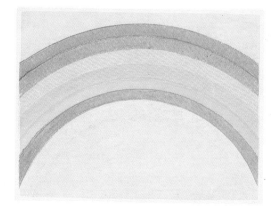

To Fred Levy

One day Bear looked out his window and saw
a rainbow. He had never seen a rainbow before.
To Bear it looked like the sky was on fire.

"Oh, my goodness!" called Bear to his
friend Little Bird. "Just look at the
sky!"
Little Bird flew over to Bear's window.
"Why, it's a rainbow!" said Little Bird.
"Come on! Let's go find the pot of gold."
"Pot of gold?" said Bear. "What are you
talking about?"
"Don't you know?" replied Little Bird.
"They say there's a pot of gold at the
end of the rainbow."

"What nonsense!" said Bear. "The sky is
on fire and all you can talk about is gold!"
And he picked up an empty honey pot
and ran outside.

At the pond Bear filled the pot with water.

Then he ran toward the rainbow.

He ran and he ran and he ran.

"Look, Bear," said Little Bird,

"the rainbow ends right by that hollow tree."

But Bear wasn't listening.
He was busy climbing a hill.
When he got to the top,
he threw the water at the rainbow.

Just then the rainbow faded away.

Little Bird chirped,
"Look, Bear, I found the gold."

Bear went to the tree.

Inside he found lots of *golden* honey.

He filled his pot...

...and took it home.

That night Little Bird came over.

Bear made honey cakes.

After dinner they went for a boat ride.

For a long while they were very quiet.

Then Little Bird said, "So it *was* a
rainbow, and I found the pot of gold!"

"Oh, no, it wasn't," replied Bear.
"It was a sky fire...

...and I put it out!"